Flowers on a Train

Flowers on a Train © 2025 Laurel Benjamin

Cover art: Megan Merchant "Garden" (USA) 2024
Cover background: iStock–AppleEyesStudio
Author photo: Dan Dickinson

ISBN: 978-1-962405-26-3
Library of Congress Control Number: 2025939495

Sheila-Na-Gig Editions
Russell, KY
Hayley Mitchell Haugen, Editor
www.sheilanagigblog.com

Flowers on a Train

Poems

Laurel Benjamin

Sheila-Na-Gig Editions

Acknowledgments

Many thanks to the editors and staff of the following journals in which some of the poems in this book appeared, often in earlier forms:

Adelaide Magazine: "The Blue Moss Sings a Song of Its Own"
Around the World Landscapes and Cityscapes: "Dispatch From the Salish Sea"
Banyan Review: "May on the Big Island"
Barzakh Magazine: "Ginko"
Bending Genres: "A Different Wish"
Black Fox Literary Magazine: "Detained for Shoplifting"
Burningword Literary Journal: "Train Ties"
Dodging the Rain: "Cannibal," "Dear Beethoven," "Effect of Rain," "Our Own Patois," "Self-Portrait as Hieronymus Bosch's *Last Judgment*"
Eunoia Review: "hiking in a storm," "What Is the ratio"
Ekphrastic Review: "Dispatch From the Nuns," Winner Lucky 7 Contest; "Empress of the Blues," "Ex-Voto to the Watermelon of Forgiveness," nominated for a Pushcart Prize; "Thermocouple"
Evening Street Press: "Missing in the Canyon"
Flapper Press: "Flowers on a Train," "Inside Bird," "Sketchbook of the Alexander Valley," nominated for Best of the Net
Flash Boulevard: "Instruction Book for Working at A&W"
Glassworks Magazine: "Self-Portrait With Flesh"
Hare's Paw Literary Journal: "To a Harbor Seal"
Lily Poetry Review: "Giantess," "Visionary," "While She Blotted Her Lipstick"
LIT Magazine: "Waiting for Leonora Carrington at the Café Alma Negra"
Lothorien Poetry Journal: "Shedding Her Skin"
Minyan Magazine: "In the last conversation with my father we talked not of birds,"
Mom Egg Review: "Brushed"
Nixes Mate: "After Hearing Mark Doty Discuss His Poem 'Brilliance'"

One Art: "Searched"
Pendemics 2024 E-Journal No. 5: "Elegy for the Blanket Man"
Pirene's Fountain: "Away From the Nest," "Sketchbook of Delft"
Sheila-Na-Gig online: "Tearformation," "Self-Portrait of a
    Hurricane"
The Inquisitive Eater: "We Bought Bagels With Our Cousins in
    Jersey"
The Shore: "She springs from fissures,"
Sky Island Journal: "They Stop the Seasons"
Stone Poetry Journal: "Oracle for Normalites"
South Florida Poetry Journal: "Before Night Ends"
West Trestle Review: "The Bird Men"
Word Poppy Press: "onetwelveandtwo," "Tightened for Escape"

Dedications

Gratitude to so many.

Thank you to the community of writers for their support, friendship, and inspiration–

Special thanks to Hayley Mitchell Haugen, Founder and Editor at Sheila-Na-Gig Editions, for your belief in my voice, selecting the manuscript for publication, and bringing this book into the world.

Eileen Cleary, mentor and teacher, for your critical feedback and teaching moments, from the first.

Sandra Fees for eyes on the manuscript in various stages, and so much support and friendship.

Lisa Alletson, Jo Ann Billodeau, John Sibley Williams for early eyes on the manuscript.

Megan Merchant, for your revision workshop and eyes on a few pieces in the manuscript to that end, which informed my process.

Jennifer Martelli, for inspiring me with your writing and I've learned so much.

To my Ekphrastic Writers group for your constant support in a safe space: Doris Ash, Donna Carnes, Annis Cassells, Susan Michelle Coronel, Gabby Davoy, Joanne Durham, Adrienne Drobnies, Sandra Fees, Michelle Holland, Lynne Kemen, Kila Knight, Marzena Lesinska, Jennifer Martelli, Megan Merchant, Marina Richie, Julia Ross, Rebecca Surmount, Suzanne Van Leendert, Lois Perch Villemaire, Julene Waffle.

Thanks to my critique group: Lynne Kemen, Marzena Lesinska, Rebecca Surmount, and earlier on, Anastasia Vassos.

To Lorette C. Luzajic: for your workshops, inspiration, and for setting the ekphrastic fire.

Thanks to Toni Littlestone for your warmth, courage, and faith in life, in our writing group.

To Lilly-Marie Lamar, dear friend.

To Lynne Kemen, my writing partner. Thank you for your humor, wit, and enthusiasm.

To my brother Mark Benjamin: inspiring me creatively.

To Dan Dickinson: grateful for your love, companionship, and support which made this book possible.

Contents

Negotiating for the Dandelion

Sea of Flowers

My life is the gardener of my body. The brain—
a hothouse closed tight
with its flowers and plants, alien and odd
in their sensitivity, their terror of becoming extinct.

— Yehuda Amichai

Sketchbook of Delft

—after Johannes Vermeer's *The Little Street*
(View of Houses in Delft)

Brick buildings dawdle and door frames
can be counted on for their white paint
in the soft air of February, and a few leftover

thorns grapple up two stories. In the corridor
a woman bends with her broom, hips
shimmy side to side, then freeing her hands,

she picks up something she's found. Shutters
of the house are closed. I sit across the street
at a metal table with salt and pepper shakers,

napkins pink and blue like children almost
born. A bowl of salad hums with citrus
segments. A couple forks each other portions

from their plates as if they've spoken
each other's words in a ceremony, and I wonder
what kind of wedding cake they ate.

Most of my trips here have come with rain,
chasing make-believe translations
since I don't know the language. After lunch

I walk past a mother sitting sideways
on a park bench combing her daughter's hair,
fingers separating long brown waves

into braids. French accent, consonants lightly
touched. I think of yesterday when my mother
told me the news. Count how much longer

distance can provide indemnity against
my father's diagnosis. Or is it immunity
from red tulips sold in corner stands

that will make everything right? How much
longer will he live with the knowledge
that I disobey his advice? One rain drop

then another. Any minute small gaps
will fill the alleyways of afternoon.

Rose the Birches

Away From the Nest

So I can catch when blue segues
to orange, I'm waiting for the birds

to sit still. They dance the tree
with its dry seams, branches turned to leaves

like a glove ripped apart. One way or another
I'll catch them at it. Wait for the soft,

wavering *kew* in succession. For something
to happen that doesn't tear.

I think of Santa Cruz, how they're planning to repair
the coast drive, won't give up despite

earthquake faults and how cliffs comprise
sand, rock, and veins. I'm a sucker too.

In another life my cottage on a cliff
overlooks the waves, an isolated beach

where I slide down crayon mud, alit
by a negative field of lightning.

Sure, it's a dream. Could be drawn by a child.
I understand halfway mentalities.

Now I keep timing rivers with the moon's
naked heels. Something I learned

in playwriting about the second climax
of a drama. Years ago, I fractured a man

with his own non-stop language,
heaved my shoulders into a butterfly.

Disappeared.

When I return to the bluebirds,
I find their pencil beaks

plucking insects.
Then the song again.

They can't hesitate, can't soften
their parting words—

che-check.

Giantess

—after Leonora Carrington's *The Giantess*

I heard the silent trumpets of pelicans, then the line
broke and their beaks rummaged
        in my towel, soaked me

as I was already soaked
        then wrapped, tangerine bathing suit
    engraved with hieroglyphs. Then the line
broke and the waves were a code

        or was it my friend
           panting to avoid a sneaker wave,

holding a beer bottle. I learned to gossip
            these afternoons,
      but couldn't find my way back,

like the fishing boat we saw ministering oars
    narrow as ankles,

      prow out of vision.

    I wondered if they were the same men hidden
      in dunes early morning
        when my running shoes clipped
           the fog
to draw a straight line

    but broke it.

      Another friend lay out on a beach blanket

        welcoming sun to her pale skin.
    My contact lenses
reflected images
      so I saw the reverse—

                    a giantess
          whose eyes looked small-smashed
on sunburn. I saw
          a premonition of how

the line would break
          and I would leave the city.

Didn't see girlishness, didn't see the truth,
          that I couldn't make it with shit jobs
     like ABC Legal and the flower shop.

                    I saw arms like sonnets,

rhyme and meter dressed in olive skin,
          islands joined by an isthmus.

Effect of Rain

Before I spear-dived into lakes, chased drops of rain
into rivers, cupped my hands where fish swarmed,

uncatchable, my father used a pole then pulled trout
off the hook. But he is gone, didn't have to watch planes

crash into towers or a president's treason, and these
are what I time-test. And still, I've held my hands out

when it rains, listening to garments sewn of clouds,
followed drips catching birch leaves. Swum in lanes

wearing spandex with green curlicues. Sewed a skirt
and cape from mesh, attached sequins, a dryad's wardrobe

where the air breathed in. And still I ask, could I stop
the past, my father seizing up on the car ride from LA—

what in the fish he caught would have taught me.
I've swept away algae that masks the depths,

but it's not the same. If I could, like my father, I'd return
a rain jacket to REI after two years, or find the one thing

missing in the garage. How he rested an eye
on his patients, counseling them towards reconciliation.

He taught me before I was born which way
north lies and where cuts in a map reveal a stream or a lake.

Visionary

We owned the night sky
as my brother snuck out
and five minutes later I followed

to avoid our parent's radar.
What did we fear—
father's analysis, the Rorschach blots,

mother's card catalog schedule
and neatly buttoned shirtwaist dresses
slipping us into slots?

My brother saw circles, snails, wheels spinning.
He traced them with his index finger
as if his cornea contained a telescope.

Brother, did the stars cast a spell,
you who spent years in special schools
reversing letters in words?

He mapped constellations
while I played hangman
in the back row of geometry.

On a Sierra Club trip we lay our bones
against granite boulders
as the leader introduced the Western sky

where light beams
fell to earth.
Star upon star.

If we stayed long enough
we'd find what we'd need—
patch of orange and purple,

a swatch of cool green. Courage
for when the stars faded.

While She Blotted Her Lipstick

I wish my mother had been more precise like the photos in her head
of her mother and the brownstone. Or had turned her pocketbook

inside out on the mosaic coffee table, ingredients like seafoam,
murky then clear. Or in a major key she had praised

my Telemann solo, but that would have broken me. On my own,
I learned to scow through what could be had cheap,

and in garrulous form ignored the absolute, but I could not pierce
the cry of a gull as it threw its breast forward or lunge of a scorpion.

I wish she had ceased-fire the missiles she couldn't resist
so I could rest my hand in hers before the stroke, not after.

Ginko

I wish I could read water levels when the estuary
      shifts. Floods along the coast, I can follow.

Rushing water turned pink like lipstick, algae
      loosening colors. Clarity is to be envied

when houses drown in mudslides, push off
      their foundation.

Last month I saw a yellow tree.
      Every time I walked past, *jingle jingle*

sounding like coins. With each approach
      I held my breath.

Held my abdomen, where they would remove
      the mass. The leaves

twirled then straightened,
      as if afraid of scraping branches.

The tree held me in its gaze,
      then divided into three trees.

Every day on my walk. And after surgery
      when I made the one block to the tree,

a voice said,
      You will heal.

I thought, if I had ten cameras, I could create
      a wardrobe of reflection.

ballad of mothers

i've named each switchback :: cornered
the swivel :: seeds dispersed in boot laces

nursing the next generation :: dirt-clogged

up the trail towards white-capped
nurses :: over boulders

the lake offers no nursefish dogfish
dry-nurses a vibrato :: nuptials the soil

parsed fungus :: don't give up
the nurslings who've fallen :: jasper

their spiked limbs :: triangle leaves
to the ground :: deer wet-nurse

spotted babes
soft yellow bark peel :: tremolo nests

mountain turbulence :: rose the birches
gave the forest a name

Shedding Her Skin

When I reached the west coast of Ireland,
land green with the dolmen,

a kind of burial, a boat tipped for the island
where limestone disappeared onto the sea

then reappeared when we docked at Inis Mor.
A seal raised her head

where they caught seaweed in cages
and near the clochan, beehive huts.

All my hopes caught up in spring flowers—
would they bloom next year, reverie more familiar

like the back of a claw—no, softer,
the idea of returning home where I buried

my mother. Father's plot one up
and one over, Veteran's plaque and fifteen years settled.

Then home again, as I look to the selkie in my garden,
solo fox sparrow with speckled lines

along her breast, scuffs against the leaves—
she could be my mother,

mouth open for a minute, eyes alert.
She could be a dream landing on our shores.

Hunger for Blue Petals

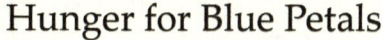

Lower Your Eyes

—after Johannes Vermeer's *The Art of Painting*

Clasp the book in your left hand.
Hold the horn, then blow.
Don't look at the map.

My calves strain, standing in this position
yet it's the softest work I've found—
no scullery, cloth wringing, child tending.

Sometimes he speaks of new neighbors
and their baby, hauling a piano to the top floor,

huffs about the demand to include tulips
in his work, these fashion gluttons.

One afternoon, I leave the studio. Dip
my toes in a canal. Loosen my bodice.
A man on his barge laughs, *Your baptism?*

In master's studio, a blue silk robe hides
the silt on my legs, a tanner's hat covers
my sticky curls.

Maybe I'm his daughter.
I don't mind if my backbone
holds in one position.

I want to cry like a peacock.

The Blue Moss Sings a Song of Its Own

—after Inka Essenhigh's *Blue Moss*

Distracted by hunger   for blue petals
      serrated and segmented   fur coat

          against the roof   of my mouth.

     The yellow lily draws air   to its candle
waves flapper tassels

        of its dress   lemon scent
     and citrus pucker

among bitter roots   fungus a blur
            where a dead vole lies.

     Grasses like tentacles   taste of almond
with finger chopsticks.   I eat the stem

        until none remains.

Climb the hill   claw through pines
           better the flat land

     the curve   bottom of a hovel inside a log
          where brightness

     cannot follow

where the blue moss
     sings a song of its own loss.

Empress of the Blues

Singer with the combo, her riotous pheasant stance
        hypnotizes the room, how Dante

could have taken her as his Beatrice
        if he'd written to-date. Her skirt an abstract

painting of canary yellow, nose separating
        from face the way tectonic plates

smolder early on a dry earthquake
        morning. During the set break, we step

outside into the dense marine layer,
        when my boyfriend jokes, *She's too loud,* his cousin

from Chicago at this San Francisco club. A foghorn
        blares, reminder from late last night

when its insistence slithered into his parent's
        basement where I slept, not allowed in his room.

Then his cousin starts the second set—
        Lady Be Good—her rouged cheeks and straight

bangs toss right to left. I know that nothing survives
        if it doesn't smolder, should follow

her example, get up on stage and call a tune,
        and they'll follow.

Waiting for Leonora Carrington at Café Alma Negra

—after Leonora Carrington's *Dark Night in Aranoë*

Your coffee tastes probably run to extremes, so I won't order for you.
Heard rumors about your cloistered artist ways,
how you grabbed a sack and threw it, and as it dripped
over the threshold, a creature with fangs
and octopus eyes birthed.
This place has a steel reputation. I can imagine
dark roast, though art photos plastered on the walls don't jive
with your paintings, especially the mohawk woman.
I expected your small frame to flame the table
right on time, but no worries—I've brought a notebook, brought
forgiveness to your smears of gold eagles, stoic edifice
despite two convent schools expelling you.
My tea bag on the saucer has begun
to cry black tears,
but no worries—I'm becoming an ecstatic
picturing your lace-deep sockets, swoosh of cotton hair.
First time in Mexico City,
hoping you'll escort me to bronze statues with frothing mouths
or an invite to a night sky party
where you'll trace tiny musical instruments the rest of us
can't see, spider-woven. All I ask, entrance into
the secret society, where I'll initiate
without floating my own secrets, though if I must,
whisper in your ear the seriousness of love and how I don't know
if I'll ever lean on anyone again. Still, I wear
my favorite lipstick. Now, just outside the door, a skunk
turns the corner to Alvaro Obregon.
And I wait.

Instruction Book for Working at A&W

At 6 a.m. I leave to catch the N-Judah streetcar. We call it
"The Worm" because its belly snakes along the tracks as if it
needs no nourishment. Takes a full hour to arrive at Union
Square. I serve the masses at A&W. A rock promoter in a
shiny tan leather jacket with epaulets, eyes glazed, orders
our version of an Egg McMuffin. Like a sacrament, he takes
the tray, touches my fingertips. Promises a seat at the next
show. The managers make us wear stockings and a skirt that
falls just below the knee. I'm empty to the bone making
sugar-free root beer floats for myself on break and slurping
them down. By the time I hop out the front door into the
touristed street my stockings are torn. The ding of the cable
car, the flower man hawking, and the business crowd on
their afternoon break. I'll be home by 4, even if I exit the
streetcar early and dive into the Chinese bakery on 24th and
Irving. No book could instruct me on how to fill my hunger
with egg custard.

Self-Portrait With Flesh

Your hips are as wide as your grandfather's,
said my mother, whose breasts pointed then sagged

like any woman. She took to Overeaters
Anonymous, no ice cream in the freezer, her favorite

curtailed, so she would fit into her gloves, particular
for small hands. She preferred butterbrickle

or cashews with ribbons of caramel bowed
and unraveled, as she stood in front of the mirror.

In the end, I inherited her gloves, crocheted hats,
stockings for skin a pale shade. In her craving

for order my mother frequented museums,
perpendicular lines funneled into a next room,

each painting or sculpture with its own identity
card describing details beyond the eye's reach.

Each craving had its own purpose,
yet she had only one way out

after I was born, when she terminated
the lump within, unseeable

from the outside, my father finding
a doctor who would perform the task.

Women are bought and sold, our bodies argued
in the highest courts, beyond flesh. Onlookers

the deciders, each of us in our own portrait
displayed, where one woman's eyes bug out

at the disgrace of ample flesh, another observing
a small landscape painting.

In that window you can see me boxed
in an ornate frame, ready

for sale. I've paid the price, stealing orange cake,
crumbs dropping along the sidewalk.

Across the street, the candy shop just opened,
but don't be distracted by tiny chocolates—

look at my thighs,
gloves not enough to cover.

Regard me as a portrait of skin and pulp,
what's inside unsacred.

We Bought Bagels With Our Cousins in Jersey

The woman who sold them wore a thick sweater
buttoned in the middle of 90 degree heat.
      But we didn't notice,

reaching for the salt shaker on the counter then opening
our mouths wide to the boiled
and baked dough,
          once a field of grain
now enclosing cream cheese pinked by lox.

     We sucked the dough before it stuck
to the roof of our mouths,

        then ran back on streets
wide enough to nourish birches planted before
foundations were metered and bricks laid.

The heat always stayed, metal to touch.

     The earth welcomed us
squawking raw and sweet from finches overhead.

Our cousins said to us, *You have no accent*
at these Jersey reunions with great aunts and uncles
who left Poland and the Ukraine.

        Like Tessie who stayed up until 3 a.m.
baking rugelach and serving us kasha varnishkas
loaded with butter.

I knew her sisters sold their wedding rings
     to bring her over.

Yet for us the war had been replaced
by Hogan's Heroes, the same way a remnant onion
on a sesame bagel

       called backwards,

the same way we didn't consider the bagel woman
and how her accent
          betrayed everything she escaped.

Ghosts in the File Room

Photos learned how to drag themselves from their sleeves
and onto the linoleum as the firm plumped themselves
off court cases on IUDs, women who discovered a hidden

defect in the crab shell, plastic prongs brittle-broken.
As we filed folders away, stories splayed on the floor—one woman
who bled unconscious and another whose device lodged

in her uterus. Photos screamed, *You don't work in the biggest*
law firm on the 30th floor of the second tallest building in the city
by accident, so we memorized, pulling cases for our lawyers,

and never stopped until the bell sounded and we punched out.
Exiting the side door onto Sacramento, we poured
into the bar across the street, elbows on rickety tables,

wood that must have been hollowed out, asking each other
how many late nights did we need to stop the images?
Sometimes I followed the receptionist to her incense-laden

apartment where we'd dance with outstretched arms, MTV videos
our absolution, knowing for each of us, the fleshy warm
place inside our bodies was secure, sacred. I left my friend late,

then back across the Bay with the Walkman plump against my ears.

Dispatch From the Nuns

My father returned with nuns' stories
from counseling sessions. Nuns slipped from
headdresses, veiled at the waist, veiled at the eyes.

They rounded names and dates in generalities
to avoid suspicion, drowsy in blue charcoal
from extra duties. *Backwards*, he said.

Sharpened shears for trimming vines
hidden in their robes. But what could they do,
except slice morning oranges, chant

in the chapel. How did they take it,
bone-tattered from standing long hours
laundering. To mend priests' garments

they wrapped thread tight around their nails,
cuticles nibbled until, like a lit sparkler,
bright red dribbled a torrent.

My father called it the machine of the church,
yet he didn't say it was nothing compared
to our family. My brother and I scribbled

notes of our own, figured we got it right in case
something happened, like solving a mystery.
One night we saw our father crumpling paper

from his pocket so made up a story,
how he'd have to climb the black oak
at the diocese campus. Well-rounded trunk

surrounded by long arms of blue oaks.
After all, *Make someone talk* was his bark
from training. Yet two years after, he admitted

he'd underestimated the church. His briefcase,
a numbered lock, kept their secrets.
Even years later I cannot open it.

Cannibal

Once, I stared so hard at a girl, I made her wet her pants.
    I'd chosen her as my nest mate, canoed

across the lake, and in the mess hall we ate off
    melamine, unburdened family stories.

Then I lied about how the girl lashed out. After,
    I tethered to new friends during the two weeks

of Girl Scout Camp, while others patted my back
    like I'd won a prize of having to put up with

something intolerable. Back home, I looked at my brother
    sideways. He hit me. He got into trouble.

But it wasn't the same as the girl at camp and the hunger
    she made me feel. Now, I can admit,

I felt afraid of my own stare like a cannibal
    forced to wait for its next meal.

No grayness, first child hiding in her pink
    room painted peach. I cringe

thinking of the girl's short straight hair, soft eyes,
    pale skin, sweatshirt frayed at her thick neck.

Self-Portrait as Hieronymus Bosch's *Last Judgment*

Back-carry me in a teacup with other male
nudes, fly swat me with your blue hoodie
                                    and red pants,

wash the floor with skirts
                    hitched up,
              because I've got nothing to lose.

    You knew
we'd never listen to global warming,
                          war-tinged diatribes.

    Christian bible me
                    into hell, no Dante-esque
              middle path desired.
Fit my head with a bird cage,

put a barrel over my middle
                    so I can roll
              metal-mouthed.

    Wrestle me with a wood-handled
knife to cut off limbs or leave me
                    standing idle
                          while a soldier

              thrusts a sword
through my bare back.

    And for once, please give me some answers.

Why didn't the woman in green smile back?

    Sure, I hate crowds but mood
                    is changeable.

I never considered the rocking chair
     would engulf me
         with unclouded and unblurred lines—

    nothing but crisp fine boundaries of objects
       touched with enough light
           to eye pop against
      the black base.

I taste the roasted garlic Bosch ate
     with dinner, washed with tannic wine,
hear his wife's bell rung
        as the studio door closed.

    My last request—banish me from this canvas
and I promise not to copy
        the red clog with a sailcloth,

    promise not to perfect my thieving ways
because believe me, we've got to look forward.

In the Slender Stalk

What Is the ratio

between seeds and vegetables, between survival
and listening, and how do we thank the right
bird for the gift? I review the method for increasing

the weight of flour metrically while cookie making,
learn how Julia Child regretted leaving her scales
behind for pounds to assuage America's kitchens,

though she knew in her gut she was right. I can't study
moon phases myself, but watch a science video
from 1962, foam-cardboard planets constructed,

imagine myself white coated, dreaming of equations
and space, designing the future. But there's so much
I don't know, how false starts prepped better materials,

rockets to the moon an exactitude. Today,
I listen to silverware found at the antique store, bend
my arms to curlicues conversing about half moons.

If only I'd baby sat, had a baby, I'd know if converting
breast for pacifier, the composition of formula
exacts the same result. Last night on tv news

they announced that concealed carry laws have come
to my area, and I ask, what is the ratio between
murder and crossfire. If a body falls long and hard

to the pavement, does it find a comrade's arm?

After Hearing Mark Doty Discuss His Poem "Brilliance"

In my own story, I'm in a surgery waiting room
with the man who would become
my husband as we dead-eye

the aquarium's girth, where one big gray fish
swooshes from end to end
and mollusks hide, and the tetras, far

from their native home, flash
thin blue-red lines.

But the goldfish.

Almost invisible behind spiny plants
so we can barely detect its mouth blowing
love-pushes. And the man who would become

my husband, he with early-stage cancer,
cannot compete with the goldfish as we readjust
ourselves on metal framed chairs.

And I have to tell you.

Hearing you discuss your friend's decision
on whether or not to buy a goldfish and
about how distance balances sentimentality

and how everything but the fish
uses plain language, and furthermore,
how the fish's overabundance steals

the show—I didn't immediately
consider the fish in my own story. Not just

the big fish, back and forth, the mollusks,
the tetras. But the bright shiny
wedding dress of a goldfish.

Detained for Shoplifting

Hands in pockets, bare legs on a metal chair,
I crossed my feet in the manager's office,
really an employee break room, water cooler

sloshing as a woman filled a paper cup
for herself. Someone's perfume
smelled like spring blooms between tracks

where my mother and I would cross
on our way to Montgomery Wards,
when she listened for the train

then led me by the hand. But this was not Wards
and my mother was not here. Nothing
sandwiched itself between the striped shirt

stuffed in my shoulder bag and the questions I had
of my future. No one asked. A man
ushered me out and into the police car.

Weight of greasy handcuffs a singular flutter.
Revving of a reborn engine, tinted
windows, radio codes I had no key for,

and the overhead light. A vague caw
from the seat where torn upholstery chafed.
And though I could not see them,

music of sharp stars pierced while a stray
hair unreachable
inserted itself under my glasses.

Dispatch From Jazz

At a New York club, I counted the three feet away
from my seat to Woody Allen as his band delivered a range
of mother-of-pearl to wood.

He lived and died in these 20 minute sets
of Bechet and Bix, where the clarinet mouthed
a small round opening,

oranged to the sax's limelight.

The club's music traveled to Paris of the 20s, sweet tea and hooch.
Josephine Baker shimmied
in a flapper dress,

arms coaxing us to dance, feathers
erect on her head,
stuffed swans on stage. She levitated off the platform,

spread her feathers, twisted her torso in time with the maracas.

I stepped outside where sidewalk vents of curlicued
metal spoke of the past, saying, *You must try Pigalle—*

Somehow it was not enough, the differences from back home—
no, not that—
too much had changed,

one boulevard easily confused with the next,
wet streets echoing buildings,
echoing themselves.

Past old Metro stations and rounded curbs where café chairs
were locked or emptied, I hoped

for a lot more. Daylight
through the wet park, past the Orangerie, without music,
without blurry lights, yet the rounded shapes of bushes

signaled how the notes once sounded.

Missing in the Canyon

In this slender stalk we listen
for my brother, our shadows leaving
a dance on the red walls

sky to ground, my parents and I,
as we replay his childhood.

We call his name—
a boomerang-echo back.

Sandstone colors open like tulips, edges
peeling back to reveal pink.

Kneeling, we sweep ashes of a tiny fire, holding
his return possible in these hours.

We're told they have a man down there,
will find him.

But this doesn't stop my father
from wringing his handkerchief
and my mother from staring off to the side.

When my brother saunters back up
chewing a red apple from a stranger,
his eyes glassy,

he shrugs as if nothing happened
and the sun,

already low in the canyon,
winks.

May on the Big Island

We drive through coffee country, take the long way
past leathery palms and small grocery stores, plenty of time

to make our flight out of Kona. At a stop sign we take
a breath as if toasting to the rise of green, hillsides

taking shape. And I wonder if this place could rebirth us.
What I mean is I know this is different, yet I've boasted

the same about other trips. Is it crazy to say Hawaii will
restructure our bones, or even better, give us words

that don't hurt each other? Here, we've almost forgotten
the injuries. A few days earlier we drove past the scarpa,

bottom of a ditch where firm shapes once lava
are now ashes—the familiar gut darkness—I looked away.

Then we paused at the edge of volcano flow, off-the-grid
homes occupying fresh lava, viewpoint at road's

end nothing more than dinosaur skin, the way
wrinkles develop. The island grows crusted orange

into the ocean, spreads over the settlement, while families
wait for the Honu to rise, myth of the sea tortoise.

We touched their shells accidentally while snorkeling.
Yet despite all this, we're leaving, rental car stubbornly

shaking over the dirt road as we make a detour
where the sign dictates Hōnaunau Bay,

by The Place of Refuge, stopping here because
we need more irregular shapes underwater

to carry us through—schools of yellow tang,
colony of rose coral, and the red velvet sea star.

Before Night Ends

Let me search for an exit
from a meadow of knots to crocus and lilac.

True, we must act, come out of the whirling,
admit an extinct model of daisy chains

a landslide you have to side step
before shale throws you down.

Love, we are caressed by dark webs—
look to the vanishing point where silk

weaves together, where we borrow
each other's shapes

and alter the hum of bees
when the last words of love cannot speak,

taking the trail back home
finding no words to bend

littered with stones the shape of eggs.
Two huge crows watch from an oak

whose leathery leaves begin to speak—

take my hand
remove my hand.

Searched

I have no reason to declare

the loss of my mother,

stomach turbulence

as engines roar for the flight

that will carry me to the island.

The employee pulls out packing cubes

trying to locate an offense,

zips open my toiletries kit—

What's this for? he asks of the face cream.

The one my mother used.

She springs from fissures,

an 'ōhi'a flower, native to volcanic ash,
the daughter I'll never have.

She trails a tunnel through ferns,
then out into the open.

                            I'm curious.

I've heard babies can erase the woman
like garden cuttings of new shoots.

Heard of an upside-down
ankle grabbed by a twin in utero,

outside arm pulling a puppet string.

Under birth, hard crusted lava,
I have no conversance with how tectonics

operate purely by touch.

I have never wanted something so pure.

Dispatch From the Salish Sea

Near dark, a Rhinoceros Auklet rocks on pale sand,
yellow bill with white horn, a shiny black hull.

Once, my family found a circle of young trees, leaves
pocked, soon to be extinct.

My mother said, *Like an old woman
kneeling*, while my brother and I stared

at each other. She could have seen herself
becoming diseased like the leaves.

Here, the waves roll. I can do nothing.
The bird stops rocking.

I wonder at the ways of the sea,
the ways of my mother's decisions

and my own. Should I bury the body, call
the Coast Guard? I recite aloud

to the bird, *Sweet are the uses of adversity*—
then leave. A predator will enjoy the remains.

Negotiating for the Dandelion

Tightened for Escape

The Soul has Bandaged Moments
—Emily Dickinson

I.

Derek picked me up in the bookstore
where I sat on the tall stool invoicing.
He came from Kerry.
He came from the bar next door, slurring, *Ha-ware-ya?*

We walked to the café on 24th Street and Mission
It was only a moment. He reached out,
clasped my pendant, a silver flower,
as if he originated the move.

II.

I was told my father sat in the passenger seat
next to my brother
when his body shook
and his eyes
rolled back.

The following week with my mother,
we didn't talk much. As if normal times,
we swam, ate a tuna sandwich at the Dollar clubhouse,
listened to the classical station.
We read the Sunday arts section,
the *Jewish Bulletin, The New Yorker.*

Images blurred, yet I saw my mother
pretend everything was normal,
dipped her tea bag in the mug
and then out in one motion.

I left mine in.

III.

Derek called my home phone.
I left a message. *Meet when I'm back to work.*
Despite only knowing surface details
I needed him like a snake victim
needs the remedy.

Then I got his letter.
I'm sick. I have a lot on my mind.
I don't know if it's appropriate to call.
One excuse would have been enough.

IV.

Later, I see him as I exit the bookstore,
track him as he enters the bar,
fist bumping a few Irish outside,
the usual way he has
of just enough, not too much,
bangs covering his eyes.

V.

I would not find escape, instead
learning who my mother was
without my father
how she sat in the middle of the couch
with one hand next to her.

They Stop the Seasons

I cover myself in gingko leaves, yellow triangles
wet from a hose in a dry season. Squint
through our yard—a cutout to stark naked trunks

frozen against a black background, purple floor.
Corridor of time when Japanese settled here,
left behind silkworms and indigo for greenhouses.

And past that shattered-glass era, low fences
topped with little roofs remain

along with trees, thread of blood from when whole
families were taken to local racetracks and then

to the camps.

Our neighbors at their move-in party, tight clusters
of laughter, cut down the two trees in their yard
that took 50 years to mature.

Stop the lemons, the yucca with its brusque trunk
and feather flowers, the undulating harvests,
the seasons.

Brushed

And so we argue in silent tree trunks where the owl hunkers,
shoe-horn blue. Mother, are we swerving to avoid our own claws?

I've spent hours listening for the howls, knees bent backwards. If only
we were soft pulls rather than delineated waist and hips.

If only I could ply through your feather layer. Once I found a towhee
sidewalk-smashed. Shallow breaths. Watched half-closed and

wondered why we explore beyond reach when we could preserve
the blue glow. Brushed with purple shadows, an orange tint

that can't be named. Is it endurance we seek or what follows?

Train Ties

Tumbleweeds roll where the train runs
despite all the rocks.
                    Farms, silos, industry of steam
                rising from the table of land
where workers drain a swamp, plant rice,
and fill it again.

Scale of the wounds—
call it forgiveness.
Call it dread.
Call it jasmine.
Call it an address.

Open space, even dry trees
        at the mountain base—
they too suffer their own mirror.

Call it eyelashes, moist
with their own nicknames.

        Plumes of smoke make their own
weather in the shape of a cross or is it a figure
with head and arms
        or a rocket
                raising itself
                        above the cloud shelf.

To a Harbor Seal

We missed its arrival to shore that night,
couldn't see out fogged windows from inside our room.

Breakers bashing against rock,
against seal fins.

Thick fat organs leaked on the beach,
no passers except birds with x-ray vision.

Cloud cover, rain pelt, rhythm on the roof,
should have alerted for war on the whiskered.

No access to absent stars, absent moon, absence.
And meanwhile incessant thrumming.

We couldn't hear the ocean's deep moan
or the warm blood of a seal.

Morning light revealed the gift to vultures' throats,
knitting needle beaks stealing a prize without guilt.

One-hundred-pound pinniped, life cut on the short side,
as women with binoculars jogged on the boardwalk.

hiking in a storm

poncho sprawl tucked under pines :: my brother and I
cradle where ants pour :: roots expose a thin march

manzanita knit close :: mother behind
on the trail :: her pink edges invisible through

switchbacks :: she could not burro us through
alpine flowers report clear skies

dark mass of god's hair :: pupils hard to read
can almost see :: the orange inside

circles forming :: re-forming
some clouds need cleaning says my brother

a white bird creases

The Bird Men

—after Leonora Carrington's *The Bird Men of Burnley*

They cage rare birds limping on fine sand,
then charge unsuspecting passersby to hear scattered
trills. Off-duty, feathered heads stare in fright

towards their monster keepers. Bird Men toil in black
fluted robes, flaunt magic learned from under-lords
in an ancient civilization. They caused

the Black Plague, two pandemics, countless wars,
though they're not responsible for deceit, for wives
beheaded. Can't be blamed for the practice

of quarter-drawing a man convicted of worshiping
the wrong god. The Bird Men placed a glove order
from Shakespeare's father, fine-grained

goatskin, perfect fit for an incantation
to lure beaks. We should fear their arrival in town,
long narrow snouts fitted into keyholes, scouring

birth records to read scrawled cursives of how we grew
from sparrow into human form. Stethoscope ears
hear a fast heartbeat macraméd. There are gods

we don't name, images emblazoned on shells and trunks
we can't explain. I know I'll end up knotted
and half-hitched for complaints of being human,

would cut off a Bird Man's beak rather than
suffer a spell which would turn me back.

Ex-Voto to the Watermelon of Forgiveness

—after Frida Kahlo's *Viva La Vida Watermelons*

Thanks to the saint of forgiveness for the time
I threw a ten-pounder across

a patio where it ruptured against a tree,
roots bloodied. Thanks to the flowers

that made the fruit, a scrambling
trail with keyhole leaves larger than

the head-shaped bulb. Devotion to sweet
flesh holds no hardness despite the rind,

no bitterness against internal division,
no judgment for a wild stripe

leading towards musk green,
fatty pear. My thanks are unharvested

trivial stitches that can't hold
a watermelon together,

decorative cut edges with seeds
dark enough to shine in the sun, honesty

soft-crumbled, fertility
crushed. Devotion to the prism

of forgiveness demands the north wind
wait for the harvest.

*An Ex-voto is a small devotional painting on tin in the Mexican
folk-art tradition

A Fuzzy Dot Like a Dandelion

My mother started sentences
with the word *no*.

Like boxcars she kept coming
yet I cannot plant three billion trees

in my backyard
global warming reversible.

In St.-Germain-en-Laye
walking the paths of Versailles

now part of the town
I only thought of goat cheese

raw unpasteurized with ash
a box shape

impossible for us, but cheesemakers
like palace pathmakers

even with heavy lifting
or dripping candle wax

know
things change

know
of continuance.

They did not carry mountains
up hills

did not measure too much
whey—

like a damsel fly they
engineered perfect intentions

for laws not understood.
If my mother were alive

would she attempt to reverse poison
in the stinging tree

or would she need a tollgate to get here?
Would I still be drawn to the redwood

with its canopy of creatures
or would I crawl towards

loneliness if I had the choice?
I would like to put the burned forests

back together, stumps to leaves,
give the gibbon an extra arm,

a rope bridge to swing
through the arboreal highway.

self-portrait as a hurricane

my hair reddens to the war of wild air // I pierce
through glass where a woman measures

the wrong ingredient in lemon bars // got it wrong like a novice
the bowl breaks // roiling my lust

over flooding rivers // I pour myself into the surge
drop trees // batter and trap people on roofs

dogs howl // yellow tiger lily streaks
run through green stems

I head for a beach // shred umbrellas and tables
cheerful flamingos // gone in an instant

neatly laid out highway lined with palm trees // gone
rear-end cars // glass fractured

metal crushed // over bodies doubled
bloodied

Elegy for the Blanket Man

I have no right to tell his story, how he carried his blanket
every day, hungering for vibrations of home, living
on a path stretching four cities.

This is a story of slow medicine and how that failed,
the local mental hospital closed and the one hospital with
a single-room ward. Here, he slept on the green path

under the woosh of the overhead train. He had no
1185 Park Avenue, no fingertip database to text
LMAO to his son in juvie. Sometimes he rose from his hovel

for the street groaning with parked cars and an organic market,
blanket a time-warp, shoulder frayed, pants soiled.
Neighbors use the same corridor, exercise

among clover and wild oak, and a few monkey puzzle trees
with no business growing here. Surely, this man
would have allowed a temple to wrap his slender body

in a clean cloth before the paramedics
who blared, *Casualty*, or if my father were alive
he would have chatted up the guy like he was his patient,

asked about community services. This country
is more a folktale where a choir sings *Abandon me*.
I've used a shovel, tipped dirt into my parents' graves,

held the difference between a garden trowel
and how even a small error forms an elegy.

Sea of Flowers

Thermocouple

He crouches on cement in front of our water heater,
twisting his head, flashlight clipped to his cap,
with the afternoon settling into him. And he narrates

the details like he's training me on metal-to-metal
connection, and I feel like I'm still in the machine.
Earlier, in a medical room, they locked a cage

on my head. Instructed shallow breaths. Body
pushed into a vestibule where the click clunk
reminded me of a rock concert where earplugs

did nothing. I gulped between tones, saw cubes
of blue and green and a circular shape,
each watercolored object part of something larger.

The plumber explains about the unit, inserts
screws by hand, closing the access panel
to the heater. Pushes the line aside.

He is more than one guy, navigating the industry
where turrets safeguard a citadel and a light ignited
will gift us. *Is the heater popping, tapping, rumbling?*

I wonder about the results of my MRI and whether
a brain tumor has formed, how long I have to live,
or maybe it's nerves behind the ear like the doctor said.

The plumber unwinds the new thermocouple,
threads its copper coil through the opening.
This magnetic beauty.

Oracle for Normalites

In the almost dark basement of my friend's house
we all positioned our fingertips
                  like playing the piano
                        on the Ouija board

and the table   slowly   jittered   and rose a woman
                        light as clouds
          with a veil   flitting
                            down.

A ghost sang from the screened past
                  (*My aunt,* Julie whispered)
        cadence
of two-syllable words

a man's name   pain in his heart
        she was asking the questions   where and how
                all the way from Panama.

We did not mean to erect the dead   had no gates of hell
                    over our shoulders
              brothers not old enough
      for Nam or the Summer of Love

and my mother had her finger on the pulse
           of opera, not news or pop culture.

We were Normalites   did not need an oracle
      to digest Julie's mother's
          curry chicken and plantains

grew up with bussing   did not need
        the world of spirits
               to instruct

yet we heard the message

when the table rose   high as our shoulders
                                    shaked   rattled our ears
                        full attention

we were not uninnocent.

onetwelveandtwo

My brother and I defended a fort of secret language
built on a high point, and below, the pavement
already broken as it hit
the air, our stomachs rumbling.

We were tied together with our quote book,
caught our father's late night eating
cream of corn out of a pot, until
he'd stand up and yell,
Let's go to Moscow—

sarcasm we lived on. Then we ran back
smooth as glass to our rooms
and scribbled the words.

No one knew what the phrases meant—
to us they developed into songs
on long car trips or at a campsite

where my brother drummed with sticks
on the picnic table. Some songs were meant
for our father, some our mother's thighs, others for pets.

perrythepuddlepatchpainter
foolaroundblogue
wilers or boars
falatohausen
onetwelveandtwo

We chortled the syllables
cherry picked from our storehouse
to bust each other up
in the failing light of adults.

Tearformation

—after Zhu Jinshi's *Boat* sculpture at the San Francisco
Asian Art Museum's 28 Chinese exhibit (2015)—40-foot,
Xuan paper, bamboo, cotton thread

I beg the artist showing her work
to tear and perforate me, turn me sideways.

Long to be cradled into the paper tunnel,
the hung shuddering pieces. Wished my mother

were here to sing its praises, she who calligraphied
paper, origamied paper, marbled paper.

She would have cut an ode to this beast where
people walk through, a tunnel emitting

their chatter, then gasps as they disappear.
I've questioned the way we depend on clouds' ability

to meditate with sonorous space, like a magic-trick box
suspended with the assistant inside,

magician demonstrating. No strings. No gravity.
I think, as I enter the paper tunnel,

this is my journey without my mother.
Crescendo of soft torn edges

like her homemade paper sheets,
uneven and imperfect

with nubs and whispers

of plant matter. The inside
resonates with air, in sync

with thunderous shifts on all sides,
as I make my way through.

A Different Wish

You're too afraid of who you are to know who you can be.
—Paul Tran

I cross the ghost of a truck, uprooted, outside the house where I once lived. Where a truck ponied through. I wish the porch had the power to stop lights, crushed the truck before it crushed the house, wish it could draft swear words. I walk past a man pushing a baby carriage, unbroken eyes, unbroken mouth. I've moved across town to another city where I don't have to re-grow survival, yet can't help listening to every screech, cars speeding the next block over. Back here this morning, I smell the rust of the truck, hear windows exploding, remember shutters herringboned. Close my eyes. Almost fall on the new sidewalk, a swerved shape to avoid sycamore roots.

*

You're crushed into millefiori too far to see swooshes of who you see. Blue, orange, red, the way a pool of eyes disappears. You're unworried for the next square where children kick the soccer ball, screams pulsating. You're a bowl of oranges. Cut off the eyes, unworry the nubbed surface, unsquare the courtyard tiles. You're a canal running shallow. You're a pastry shop where they sell almonds ground and frothed into heaven. A girl working at the bookstore said, when your cat dies, you'll return. Sometimes you wonder if it was just time, not some prediction. You'll never learn but you made it.

*

Yesterday, I swear I could write dialogue, where we performed in each other's short plays. Hats we took from the defunded drama department. Mine a priest talking to a nun, as far as I could get from Jewish. Fractured glasses hitting the ground when they went out for a smoke. Intermission a habit. A pool of blood on stage. That was fifteen years ago. Now I keep wondering if I wrote a different play, would I not have married, would I have completed a Ph.D., would I have opened a lasagna and chocolate cake restaurant like my brother wanted. I wonder if the genesis of poetry sits outside a broken house. If a porch light would grant a different wish.

In the last conversation with my father
we talked not of birds,

not of ribbon ignited, but the wedge of blue cheese
for his birthday. Maybe I hoped that each word,
a pyre lit at dusk, would smoke-signal our ancestors

for help with the conversation. We talked not of a turned
wood sculpture on the marble table or the painting
of blue ladies strumming guitars, not stormy grains

of fog that inhabit the bay or letters sent
about careers, snail mail voice insistent as a wren's
curved aperture, beak and tail upright. This was no spiel.

Feet did not sink into carpet, carpet did not turn into sodden
grass, did not reveal a background landscape with bridge,
only kitchen lights where Mom pulled

dinner out of the oven. We came less from a storyline—
despite Russian pogroms, an orchard bloomed past
his father's Flatbush apartment

where Yiddish-Hebrew newspapers opened
to kosher dishes, a time when young men didn't linger.
What all this means is, despite everything, that evening

we inched forward, not talking of birds, knees knobbed
against coffee table, taking turns grasping the little
knife, cutting into the smooth chunky cheese,

fire and smoke, made it an encounter. Shoulders
sloped as we chuckled, talking not of birds—
what did we talk about?

I wouldn't know you'd die four days later.

No birds. No ribbon. Only the dusk, where bare
tree arms, brown and wet, stretched for the sky.

Sketchbook of the Alexander Valley

How do I close the rain and

valley of tightly

knit fog. One stroke across your

cheek is all I have,

a few nights then gone, the rain

broken flashes. Headlights

reveal soaked wintered hills and

lichen-laced oaks.

What's falling are the many

strings of a quartet

from a Slavic land, I don't

pretend anymore, clear drops

intact on serrated leaves

as we trudge uphill, muddy

trail through mushroom-capped woods

to the fern laden falls.

Dear Beethoven

The man in the next row looks at his wife

after every outburst of the quartet and says, *Hmm*.

Tell me, what can I do? It's enough for me

after a few days of anger. But the waltz—

can I praise the violin, higher in pitch, flowerets

strewn and heroic deeds. Tell me, how did you nestle

a woman's voice in the middle of the darkest

movements? I've heard you hum over the music room.

You must have known, in the midst of the cello

deep diving. After all, light divided is still light,

both violins upward, viola holding the lines together.

Then the sotto voce, dark promise at the center

where the mind wanders without eyes, silhouetted

against stars. Tell me, your notes, half-life

of their former selves—do they signal the end

of your own life? When you walked out and through

the cypress garden with its airy pockets, opened.

Our Own Patois

Patois for snow means pines covered, needles bunched
like fur hats. My thighs have a different language

for cross-country skiing through the snow field,
as Mom and I whisk from the lodge over the entire stretch—

no traffic, no deer, even the ravens have obeyed
rules of hiding, season of naming their young months ago.

Our memory depends on birds who make sure the snow pack,
just right, depends on clear sky. At the lodge, stacked beds

tuck under earth, where the building cuts in at an angle,
not caring how the Sierras formed. With father and brother

we pitch in for meal prep or dish washing, box checked
when complete. My mother refuses to live

by another's rules, and alone in the snow, she has decided
on this route, where we proceed in silver, kissed

with sparkles. Then a moment later she sets her sights
on the warming hut, a kind of solution to a problem

I don't know, has lasted an hour, where we might be carried
out of this world. The cold. We find the door, push

with all our muscle, logs ready to be lit, sit facing
the stone hearth for giants. We pull out lunch bags—

tuna and PBJ, golden apples. She turns away from me.
Then she twists off the water bottle lid and we turn

to each other in surprise at the soundlessness.
Years later, without her, I have no choice but to trace

the patterns she set, so when I find the Sierra Club
brochure, open the well-creased thick paper,

and it tears, all I can do is read on either side, how the land
beyond the lodge is snow worthy. I draw hope

with a red pen through the empty field to mimic
the plow of our skis, where I'll find our patois.

Inside Bird

Praise to the red glass broken bird,
gold lettered, dropped by the bird-cat

who imagined flight, listened in pieces
to a broom swept ornament. My mother's bird,

a gift each year to hang on the Christmas tree,
though Jewish, this one not a wild bird,

not collapsible like her letters at camp.
I could see through the scarlet clouded bird

to the past, a message brittle-bred
like her calligraphy, curved and bent—

what was she trying to say in a gift
nodding me onward, the breakable bird

of rare blown glass, once sand, once liquid,
cooled to shape in the music of Birdland

bought at the Asian art gift shop
after a noodle lunch and paintings of birds.

She built a home of vases and glass,
shelves to see through to outside birds

but did she hear the inside cooing bird,
did she imagine the glass bird could fly?

Flowers on a Train

Flowers fall off her shirt   onto the floor
                                        turning into a sea
                        as she texts into her phone.

And because like her I've cried   under sunglasses,
                                        into my tea
                        under the shower   scalding

at the top of the steps between classes   I inhale
                                        the violet
                        the tangerine
            the rose.

Flowers fell off my skirt one Christmas
                        punch at a party
            attentions of the bass player   staggering

to get more into his glasses   I needed a refill
                        staring at white lights   hung
                                        on the kitchen's

            bare walls.   Almost   close enough.

            Then the band started up and he took his place
next to the piano   the drums
                                        and my saxophone boyfriend.

When we drove back home   over the bridge
            I compared   each   musical temperament
                        as the punch's anesthesia
                                                wore off.

            Flowers on a train, why do you cry
                        a saxophone player   or did you wake
in the middle of an impermeable song

a trembling   honeyed sweater
sunglasses on your curly crown.

Do you see me
a few seats away—
your flowers crawl

up my legs   thick velvet pile   silent wet.

About the Author

Laurel Benjamin is a San Francisco Bay Area poet, active with the Women's Poetry Salon. She is the curator of Ekphrastic Writers and is a reader for *Common Ground Review*. Journal publications include: *Lily Poetry Review, Pirene's Fountain, Cider Press Review, Taos Journal of Poetry, Mom Egg Review, Ekphrastic Review, Nixes Mate, West Trestle Review, Of the Book Literary Magazine, Deronda Review, Gone Lawn, Minyan Magazine, Eunoia Review, Moon City Review, LIT Magazine,* and *Rise Up Review,* where her work has been recognized. Her work has also been anthologized in *Women in a Golden State* (2025); *The Nature of Our Times: Poems on America's Land, Waters, Wildlife, and Other Natural Wonders* (2025); and *Turning a Train of Thought Upside Down: An Anthology of Women's Poetry* (2006). She received Honorable Mention for the Ruben Rose Memorial Poetry Competition, was a finalist for the *Cider Press Review* Book Award, and received Honorable Mention with Small Harbor Publishing. Her work has been nominated for the Pushcart Prize and Best of the Net. Laurel holds an MFA from Mills College. She is a former temp worker, children's book buyer, and community college English instructor. She invented a secret language with her brother. Learn more at https://www.laurelbenjamin.com